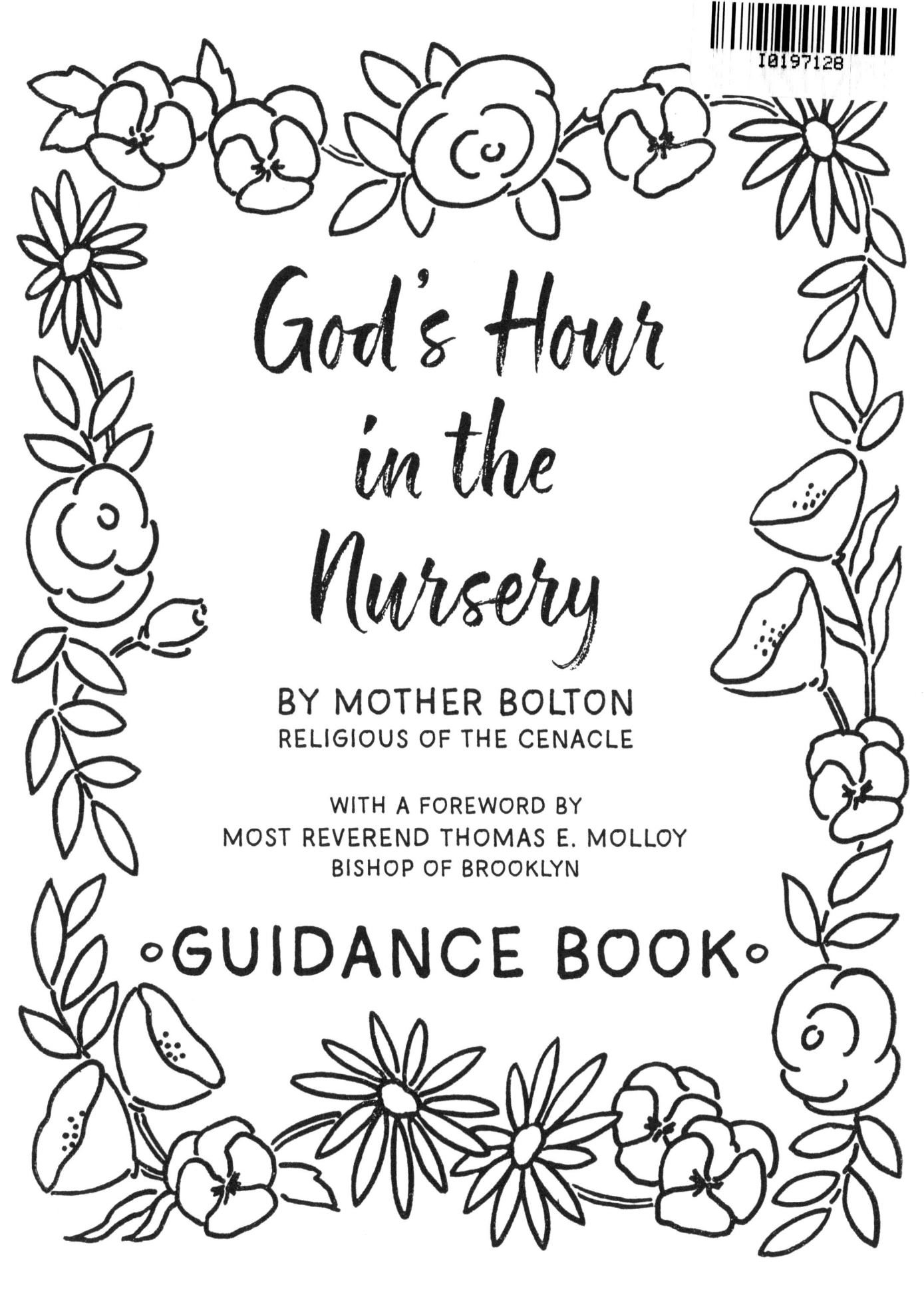

God's Hour in the Nursery

BY MOTHER BOLTON
RELIGIOUS OF THE CENACLE

WITH A FOREWORD BY
MOST REVEREND THOMAS E. MOLLOY
BISHOP OF BROOKLYN

·GUIDANCE BOOK·

This GUIDANCE BOOK is intended to be used with the ACTIVITY BOOK for *God's Hour in the Nursery.*

GOD'S HOUR IN THE NURSERY was written by the late Mother Bolton, of the Religious of Our Lady of the Retreat in The Cenacle. It has been prepared for publication by the Religious of The Cenacle, Lake Ronkonkoma, Long Island, N. Y.

This revised edition includes musical notation prepared by Sister Hunkele, of the Religious of Our Lady of the Retreat in the Cenacle, to permit the singing of the verses throughout the text.

ISBN: 978-1-64051-080-7

This book was originally published in 1947 by The Cenacle of St. Regis, NY.

This facsimile edition is based on the 1966 revised edition.
©2019 by St. Augustine Academy Press.

FOREWORD

This particular publication entitled **God's Hour in the Nursery** will have a special interest and a particular significance for many readers because it represents the final literary and educational endeavor of the late revered Mother Bolton. I venture to say that for those who were privileged to know her personally, as well as her edifying life and blessedly fruitful services, this book will reflect, in culminating expression, her deeply religious spirit and her ardent love of all human beings and especially of the little ones who are so near and dear to the Sacred Heart of Jesus.

To all, moreover, who are favored with an opportunity of reading the following pages there will come the edifying reaction that, just as the gifted and zealous authoress prayed and labored for the welfare of others throughout her vocational career as a worthy member of the Community of Our Lady of The Cenacle, so also to the end she remained true to this noble aspiration by striving to develop in the growing child a clear and correct notion and appreciation of life on three levels — natural, supernatural, spiritual or eternal.

For the realization of this worthy and useful purpose, Mother Bolton adopts most understandingly and employs most skillfully the method of telling simple stories which are gauged to a child's intelligence. And in so doing she reveals indeed true knowledge of sound psychological principles.

For instance, she gives evidence of a keen awareness of the significance of the practical similitude presented by the

Director of the Yale Clinic of Child Development in the words: "Parents and teachers who think that a child is so plastic that he can be made over by strenuous outside pressure, have failed to grasp the true nature of the mind. The mind in some respects may be likened to a plant but not to clay. For clay does not grow. Clay is moulded entirely from without, a plant is moulded from within, through the forces of growth" ("The Child from Five to Ten," by Arnold Gesell-Frances L. Ilg, page 20).

The authoress therefore is concerned chiefly in her educational endeavor with drawing out, bringing forth, developing what is in the mind, and facilitates these reactions by a process of helpful stimulation, orientation and guidance.

Then again she recognizes that the years from five to ten occupy a middle position in the span of immaturity. These years are intermediate in both a biological and a cultural sense. And she realizes that it is very necessary for both parent and teacher to know the individual and the age differences in growth processes, especially in connection with the psychology of learning, during these years. Unfortunately, in this matter many of us may be perhaps satisfied solely with the generalization that childhood is a period of seeming stability but adolescence always presents features of restlessness and disturbance. Unless, however, parent and teacher recognize the limitations of immaturity and especially facts of physical change and the development of behavior patterns in the child, they are liable to adopt false methods of instruction and harsh means of discipline.

Mother Bolton, therefore, is conscious of these requirements as she proceeds to promote in the child a knowledge of physical life, which most readily appeals to his sense perception as revealed in the great outdoors. She awakens his interest in flowers, trees, grass, vegetables and animals.

Gradually and systematically she leads the child to recognize the difference between vegetative and animal life on the one hand and human life on the other. And thus appropriately she explains that human beings are composed of body and soul and must provide not only for the needs of the body but also for the interests of the soul. And, as far as the child's limited intellectual faculties will allow, she seeks to develop the realization that a human being as a rational creature is superior to an animal. Then, more in detail, she explains that a human being is also a child of God with an immortal soul raised to the supernatural order of grace and glory. She strives to promote, moreover, some understanding of God, the Church, the Commandments, the Sacraments and prayer.

In the treatment of these religious truths the authoress makes known her conviction that religion in education is necessary not only to strengthen and perfect natural ethical and cultural development but also to ensure a proper knowledge, love and service of God; obedience to His law; horror for sin; love of virtue; and sanctification of soul.

In all her teaching processes Mother Bolton never forgets that the soul of the child comes from God and bears the Image of its Maker. The divine dignity of the child in this regard is the very foundation of Catholic education. In this viewpoint she reflects the high and holy appraisal of the child given to us by Dupanloup in these words: "The child is the human race; he is the whole of humanity; he is man. The Prince, the Priest, the Parent, the Teacher, the Magistrate, the Family, Society, the Church: all exist because of him. Moral discipline, instruction, labors, science, religion, all the rewards of toil and virtue, even divine Providence itself, all things here on earth are for him. And the reason is that he is of God and for God" ("De l'education," I, page 3).

Since this is true, the supreme law of life and the highest and holiest aim of the parent and teacher undoubtedly must be to increase the likeness existing between God and the child. And the supreme and sublime ideal of life must be for the child, in childhood, adolescence and adulthood, to realize the imitation of Christ, who is God.

✠ *Thomas E. Molloy*
Bishop of Brooklyn

INTRODUCTION

*"As to the rich in this present world, enjoin them not to think highly of themselves, not to set their hope on uncertain wealth, but rather on the **Living God**, who richly furnishes us with all things for enjoyment. Charge them to do good, to become rich in noble deeds, to be liberal, sociable, thus treasuring up for themselves an excellent foundation for the future, that they may lay hold upon what is really life."*
— I Timothy 6:17-19*

The above quotation aptly summarizes the purpose of this **Guidance Book** and its accompanying **Activity Book** for pre-school children.

The object of these books is to teach little children about the God-given gift of life.

Unit One develops in the child-mind an appreciation of the gift of *physical life* and the truth that God is First Cause of all things. The result will be, in the soul of the child, a reverent love for living things, together with prayerful gratitude to the Giver of life.

Unit Two stresses the truth that in addition to the child's physical life, God has given him a *higher kind of life,* that is, the life of his intellect and will. Through an appreciation of these gifts the child develops facility in praying and in practicing virtue.

---

*Translated from the original Greek by Very Reverend Francis Aloysius Spencer, O. P.

Unit Three gives the child a knowledge of the *highest kind of life,* that is, God's Life in him which comes to him in Baptism through Jesus, God's Own Son.

This posthumous publication from the pen of Mother Margaret Bolton gives evidence of her flaming zeal in blazing a trail for the psychological teaching of Christian Doctrine. Her earnest desire was to awaken in the souls of children at the earliest possible age the knowledge and love of God, thus ensuring "an excellent foundation for the future, that they may lay hold upon what is really life."

The Religious of The Cenacle

CONTENTS

	page
FOREWORD	5
INTRODUCTION	9

UNIT ONE

APPLE TREES	15
The Apple Tree and God (rhyme)	19
UNCLE HARRY'S GARDEN	21
Alice's Prayer (rhyme)	24
A Story	24
Daniel's Question (rhyme)	25
Another Story	25
Teddy's Answer to Patsy (rhyme)	26
Life or No Life — Which?	27
MRS. O'MALLORY'S FARM	28
Father's Rhyme about the Animals	30
Mother's Rhyme about Birds	31
MR. PERINO'S POTATO FIELD	32
The Prayer Jimmie's Mother Said (rhyme)	35
Thinking of God with Love (rhyme)	36

UNIT TWO

MORE STORIES ABOUT TREES, FLOWERS AND VEGETABLES	39
A Story	40
Billy's Rhyme about Trees, Flowers and Vegetables	41
MORE STORIES ABOUT ANIMALS	42
John's Rhyme about the Animals	44
MORE STORIES ABOUT PEOPLE	45
Joseph's Rhyme	46

	page
TALKING TO GOD	47
A Rhyme My Mother Taught Me When I Was a Little Girl	48
My Prayer	49
MORE STORIES ABOUT CHILDREN	50
Elaine's Rhyme	52
Cheerful or Sulky — Which?	52
Orderly or Disorderly — Which?	53
Kind or Selfish — Which?	55
Generous or Greedy — Which?	56

UNIT THREE

JESUS IS GOD'S OWN SON	59
THE BABY JESUS	63
Jesus Is God	64
JESUS' MOTHER	66
A Prayer	68
JESUS, THE GOD-MAN	70
Some Stories about Jesus, the God-Man	74
Lazarus	74
Two Blind Men	78
The Ruler's Little Daughter	81
The Crucifix	83
Jesus Is Alive	86
Jesus Sends the New Friend	87
Kinds of Life	88
BAPTISM	89
Jerry's Rhyme	91
Peter's Rhyme	91
THE CHURCH WHERE JESUS LIVES	92

UNIT ONE

Aim

To Develop in the Little Child

    (A) An Appreciation of the Gift of Physical Life

    (B) An Appreciation of the Truth That God Is the First Cause of All Physical Life

APPLE TREES

A LONG time ago, I met a little boy called Jimmie.
I asked Jimmie how old he was.
And he answered: "Just five."

Would you like to hear a story about Jimmie?

Jimmie lived in a big city where the houses are so close together that there are only little patches of ground where children can play.

So one day in the summertime Jimmie said to his father: "I would like to go for a walk."

His father answered: "All right. I will take you out into the country."

Then Jimmie and his father walked toward the street where the bus stopped. The bus driver saw Jimmie and his father coming, and he waited until they were in the bus.

They rode and rode for what seemed to Jimmie a long time. But at last, his father gave the signal for the bus to stop.

When they stepped off the bus, Jimmie was surprised to see only one or two little houses far, far off, and a great deal of land.

Some of this land was planted with different kinds of vegetables — tomatoes, carrots, turnips and potatoes.

But some of the land was covered only with grass.

This was the country.

So Jimmie and his father started off on their walk.

While they were walking in the country, they went into an orchard.

In every orchard there are many fruit trees.

And in the orchard where Jimmie and his father walked, there were many apple trees. For it was an apple orchard.

The apple trees in that orchard were all covered with beautiful pink and white flowers.

Look in your Activity Book for the picture showing an apple tree covered with pink and white flowers. *(page 3)**

*The page numbers in parentheses refer to the Activity Book.

Jimmie could not reach up to the pretty flowers. So his father picked a little bunch for him.

Find the picture of Jimmie holding his bunch of apple blossoms. *(page 4)*

* * *

While Jimmie was looking around the orchard, he saw one little old tree without even a leaf or a flower on it.

Find the picture of the little old tree. *(page 5)*

* * *

Jimmie said to his father: "What is the matter with that little old tree?"

Jimmie's father answered: "That little old tree has been hurt. Perhaps long ago the lightning struck it. Now there is NO LIFE in it.

"All these other trees have green leaves and pretty blossoms, because there is LIFE in them."

Jimmie said to his father: "One day when we were looking at that big tree near our house, you told me that in the beginning the big tree was a little seed that

Grandfather planted in the ground. But where did that little seed come from?"

Jimmie's father told him that the little seed Grandfather planted had fallen from another tree that had LIFE in it, but that in the very beginning of the world it was God who put LIFE into the first tree.

Jimmie asked: "Why did God put LIFE into the trees?"

Jimmie's father told him that God loves us and that He put LIFE into the trees to make us happy and to give us delicious fruit to eat.

Then Jimmie asked: "Is there any other person who could put LIFE into the trees?"

His father answered: "No one but God could put LIFE into anything.

"For God is THE GIVER OF LIFE."

Then Jimmie and his father walked out of the apple orchard. And his father said to Jimmie: "Mother will want you to tell her what you saw and talked about during our walk. So let us think about it."

Jimmie told his father all the story that he remembered about the trees in the apple orchard and about God, who loves us and wants us to be happy, and who put LIFE into the trees to make them beautiful.

Then his father said: "Would you like to hear my rhyme about the apple trees and about God?"

Jimmie said that he would like to hear it.

This is the rhyme that Jimmie's father said:

THE APPLE TREE AND GOD

Jimmie told his father that he thought Mother would surely like his rhyme, and asked if they could say it together.

So, on their way home, Jimmie and his father practiced saying the rhyme together very nicely, so that Mother would know about their walk and be as happy as they were.

Would you like to learn this rhyme?

When Jimmie told his mother the rhyme about **THE APPLE TREE AND GOD,** she liked it.

And she said: "Jimmie, would you like to make a picture telling about the beautiful trees with LIFE in them and the poor little tree with NO LIFE in it?"

Jimmie told his mother that he would like to do this. Then Jimmie's mother said:

"Turn to the first picture in your Activity Book, showing an apple tree. Now look at the tree on page 5.

"Which of these trees is the more beautiful?

"The first tree is beautiful with leaves and flowers, because there is LIFE in that tree.

"The other tree has no leaves and flowers, because there is NO LIFE in it.

"Now see if you can color your own pictures in the Activity Book. I will tell you what to do." (pages 6, 7)

UNCLE HARRY'S GARDEN

THIS story is about a little girl.

She was five and a half. Her name was Anna Mary.

One day in the summertime, Anna Mary went with her father to visit her Uncle Harry.

Anna Mary liked flowers.

So Uncle Harry took Anna Mary and her father into his flower garden.

There he showed them his beautiful pansies, poppies, roses and daisies.

Find the picture of Uncle Harry's flower garden. Which are the pansies? the poppies? the roses? the daisies? Color your own picture of the garden. (pages 8, 9)

Anna Mary thought the plants in her Uncle Harry's garden were very pretty.

He told her to pick a nice big bunch for herself, and then he said: "Be sure to put them in water, so that they will not wilt."

Look at the picture showing the flowers that Anna Mary picked. (page 10)

While Anna Mary was picking her bunch of flowers, she saw a plant that was not beautiful as the other plants were. So she called out to her father, who was sitting on a bench: "Father, look at this plant. It has no green leaves and no flowers."

Her father said: "That plant did have LIFE in it. But something happened to it. The chickens dug the plant out of the ground. Now it has NO LIFE in it."

* * *

Find the picture showing the plant with NO LIFE in it.
(page 11)

* * *

On their way home from Uncle Harry's house, they walked through a big field where there was a great deal of grass.

Find the picture showing the field where Anna Mary and her father walked. *(page 14)*

Most of the grass in this field was very soft and green, and Anna Mary knew that there was LIFE in it.

But there was one little patch of grass on top of a hill that was not green. Instead it was stiff and dry. For there were no trees there, and the sun had burned this grass until there was NO LIFE in it.

Find the picture showing Anna Mary and her father looking at that little patch of grass. (page 15)

Anna Mary said to her father: "This little patch of grass has NO LIFE in it at all. I like to play where the grass has LIFE in it."

Then Anna Mary's father told her something very important which she did not know before.

He said: "Anna Mary, God owns all the world, and I think He put LIFE in the grass and the flowers so that little children could have a nice place to play.

"God is Very Good, so in the morning — or when you are playing — you may like to whisper to God that you thank Him for the grass and the beautiful flowers. For God hears every little whisper.

"And when you think about God, or whisper or talk out loud to Him, it is a prayer."

Now suppose we make up some little prayers to God about the flowers and the grass.

This is a prayer I say:

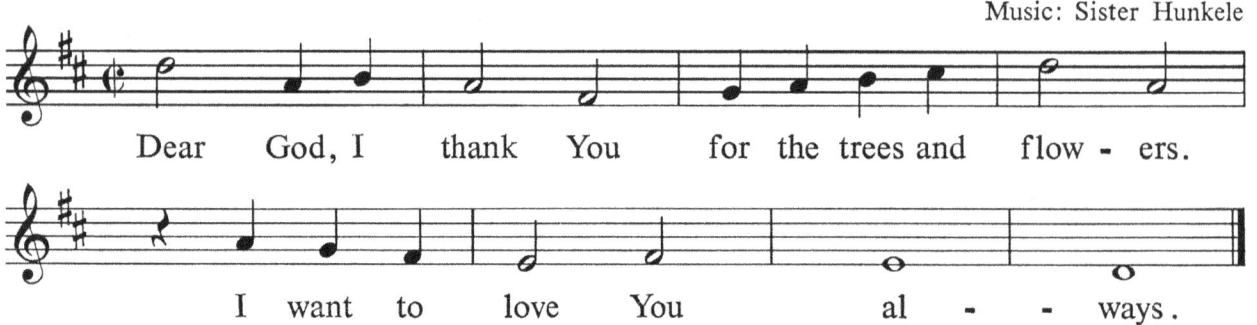

Music: Sister Hunkele

Dear God, I thank You for the trees and flow-ers.
I want to love You al - - ways.

Now, you whisper to God the prayer you like.

I know a little girl called Alice. One day she told me the prayer she says. Let us say **ALICE'S PRAYER** together:

ALICE'S PRAYER

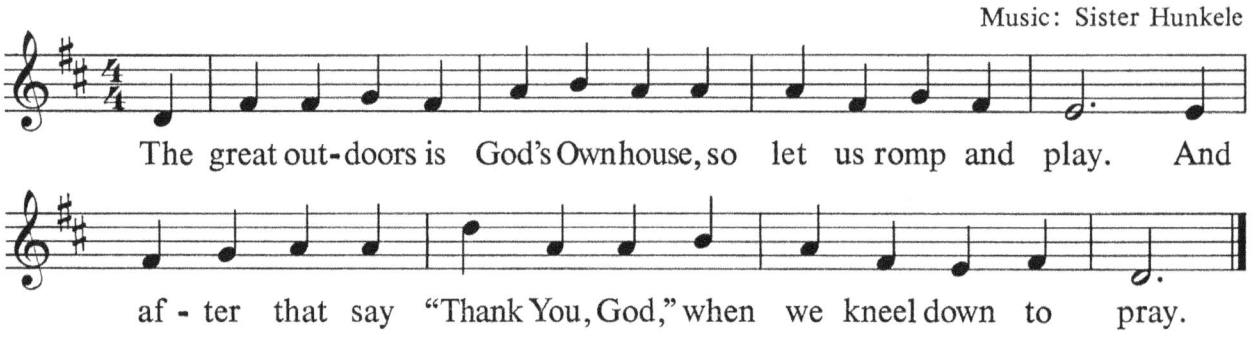

Music: Sister Hunkele

The great out-doors is God's Own house, so let us romp and play. And after that say "Thank You, God," when we kneel down to pray.

Find the page in your Activity Book that says: "Thank You, God."

Put your own colors on the page to say: "Thank You, God."

(*page 16*)

* * *

A STORY

The other day I met a little boy called Daniel. Daniel and I were talking about pretty green plants. Daniel said that he wanted some for his little garden. Then Daniel told me that he had a question to ask about the green plants. He wanted to know if I would try to answer his question. Shall I tell you Daniel's question and my answer?

DANIEL'S QUESTION

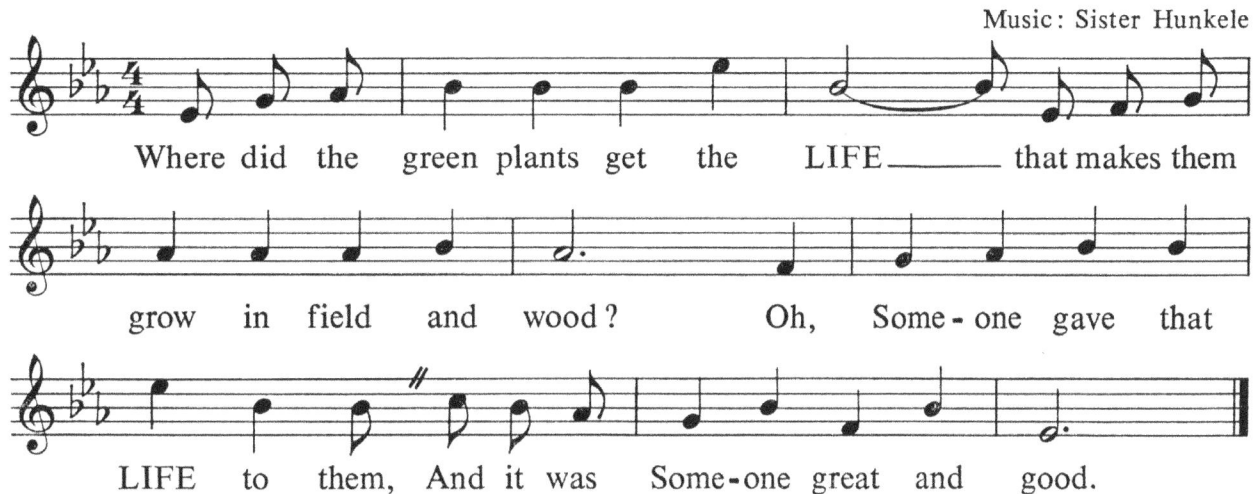

Where did the green plants get the LIFE that makes them grow in field and wood? Oh, Some-one gave that LIFE to them, And it was Some-one great and good.

Would you like to learn this rhyme?

ANOTHER STORY

Long, long ago, Teddy and his little sister Patsy were looking at some flowers in a flower garden.

The flowers were of many colors; some were blue, some were red, and some were yellow.

Patsy asked Teddy if he knew why God put LIFE into the flowers and gave them such pretty colors. This is:

TEDDY'S ANSWER TO PATSY

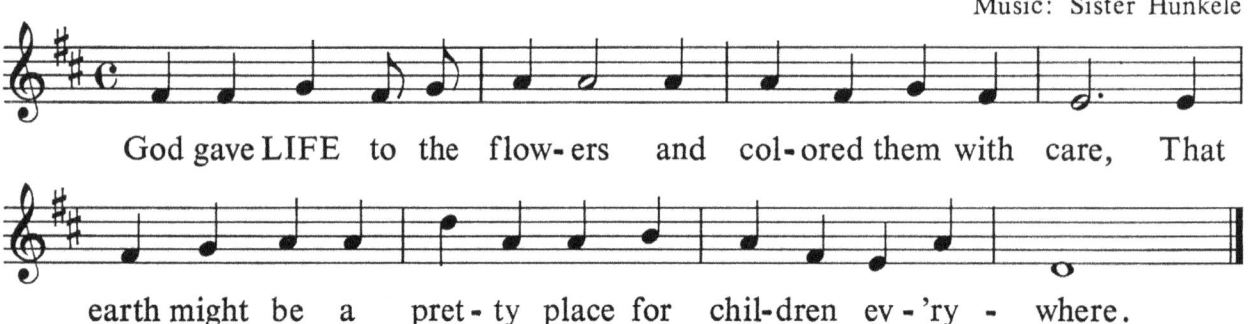

Music: Sister Hunkele

God gave LIFE to the flow-ers and col-ored them with care, That earth might be a pret-ty place for chil-dren ev-'ry-where.

Jimmie said that he would like to learn that rhyme so that he could tell it to his cousin Anna Mary when she came to visit them.

Shall we learn TEDDY'S ANSWER TO PATSY?

* * *

Find other pages in your Activity Book showing pretty flowers with LIFE in them and a poor little plant with NO LIFE in it.

Color these pages. *(pages 12, 13)*

LIFE OR NO LIFE — WHICH?

1. *The pear tree in blossom.*
2. *The tree that was cut down a long time ago.*
3. *The cedar tree all brown.*
4. *The lilac bush with green leaves.*
5. *The plant with no leaves and not green.*
6. *The sweet peas with pink and white flowers.*
7. *The pansies uprooted by the chickens, that have been lying in the sun for many days.*
8. *A lawn covered with green grass.*
9. *The roses just picked.*
10. *The roses picked a week ago.*

MRS. O'MALLORY'S FARM

JIMMIE and Anna Mary were cousins. They lived in different cities.

So one spring day Anna Mary's mother took Anna Mary with her when she went to visit Jimmie's father and mother.

They were going to stay several days.

This made Anna Mary very happy.

It made Jimmie happy, too.

Jimmie told Anna Mary that it would be fun if they could go to Mrs. O'Mallory's farm.

So Anna Mary asked Jimmie's father to take them.

And in the afternoon Jimmie's father did take Anna Mary and Jimmie to see Mrs. O'Mallory's farm.

There was a large field back of Mrs. O'Mallory's house.

And while Anna Mary and Jimmie were walking in Mrs. O'Mallory's field, picking bunches of violets and buttercups, they saw horses, cows, dogs, and many birds.

Look at the picture showing a corner of the field on Mrs. O'Mallory's farm. *(page 17)*

Find the violets in the picture. What color are the violets?

Look at the buttercups in the picture. What color are the buttercups?

Some of the animals on Mrs. O'Mallory's farm have four legs and are walking about and eating grass. What are their names?

Some others have four legs, too, but they are not like the horses and cows, and they barked as we came into the field. What are these?

* * *

You know that God put LIFE into the trees, the flowers and the grass to make them beautiful. For you have learned that God is THE GIVER OF LIFE.

So it was God who gave LIFE to the animals in this field.

And it is God who gives LIFE to all the horses, all the cows, all the dogs, and all the other animals in the whole world.

It is God who gives LIFE to the birds flying in the air.

And it is God who gives LIFE to all the fishes swimming in the rivers.

Jimmie said: "I like to learn about God."

Anna Mary said: "I love God."

Then Jimmie's father said:

"Another day we will talk more about God. But now I will tell you the rhyme I made up while we were looking at the animals."

FATHER'S RHYME ABOUT THE ANIMALS

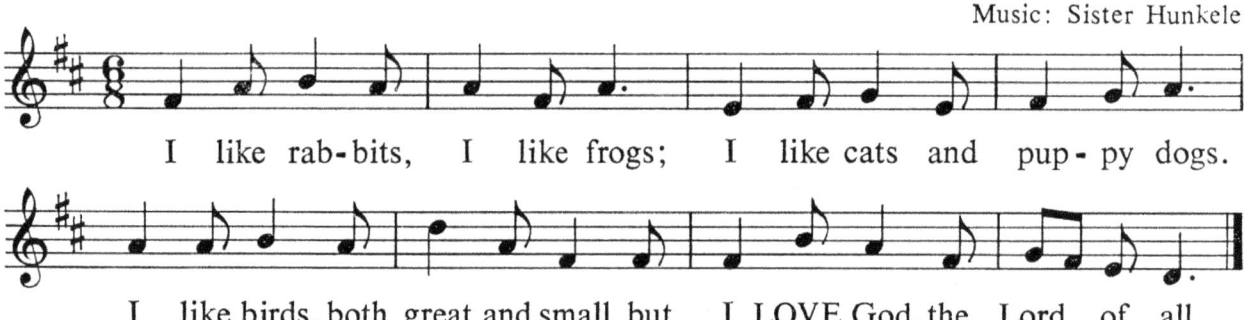

Music: Sister Hunkele

I like rabbits, I like frogs; I like cats and pup-py dogs.
I like birds, both great and small, but I LOVE God, the Lord of all.

Shall we learn **FATHER'S RHYME ABOUT THE ANIMALS?**

When the children returned home, Jimmie said: "Mother, would you like to hear **FATHER'S RHYME ABOUT THE ANIMALS?**"

Jimmie's mother and Anna Mary's mother both said that they would like it very much.

Then Father and the children said the rhyme together.

Jimmie's mother said that she did like all of **FATHER'S RHYME,** but best of all the part about the birds both great and small.

Then Jimmie said: "Mother, you say a rhyme for us about the birds."

Anna Mary said: "Yes, please do."

Then Jimmie's mother said this rhyme:

MOTHER'S RHYME ABOUT BIRDS

Music: Sister Hunkele

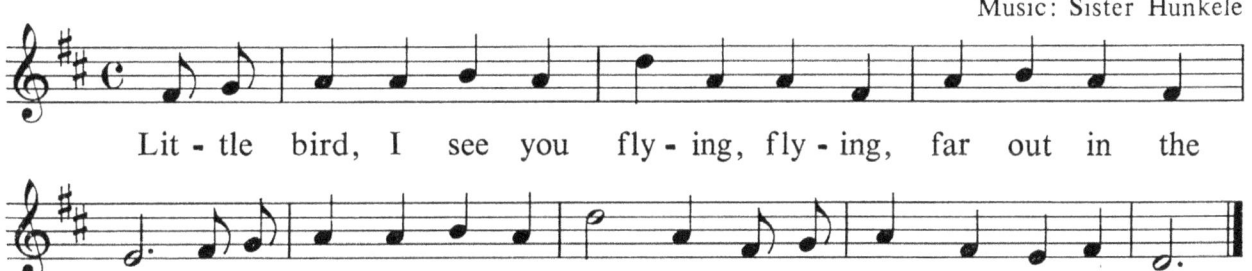

Lit-tle bird, I see you fly-ing, fly-ing, far out in the blue, And I hear you sing-ing, sing-ing, with the LIFE God gave to you.

Anna Mary said: "Let's all say **MOTHER'S RHYME ABOUT BIRDS** together, just as we did your father's."

* * *

Find the picture in your Activity Book showing LIFE in animals and birds.

Color your own page. (*pages 18, 19*)

MR. PERINO'S POTATO FIELD

A FEW days after Jimmie's father had taken Anna Mary and Jimmie to visit Mrs. O'Mallory's farm, Anna Mary's mother told the children that she would be away all day visiting some other friends.

Then the children asked Jimmie's father and mother to take them for another walk in the country.

So Jimmie's father and mother and Anna Mary and Jimmie started out together.

And after a while they came to a field where many, many potato plants were growing.

This potato field was owned by Mr. Perino.

Look at the picture of Mr. Perino's potato field.
(page 20)

Nearly all the potato plants in the field had LIFE in them.

But there were a few plants that had been eaten by little potato bugs.

These plants had NO LIFE in them.

Color your own page. *(page 21)*

While the children were looking at the potato plants, Jimmie's father said: "As we are walking through the field, do you want me to tell you more about God?"

And Jimmie and Anna Mary both answered: "Yes."

Then Jimmie's father began by saying: "Look at the men working in the field. What are they doing?"

Anna Mary replied: "They are sprinkling the potato plants."

Jimmie's father then asked: "Why do you think they are sprinkling the potato plants?"

Anna Mary said: "I think they are doing it to give the plants a good drink of water."

But Jimmie said: "Look at the bugs on those potato plants. They will take all the LIFE out of them. Then there will be no potatoes.

"I think the men are sprinkling the plants with something to kill the potato bugs."

His father told Jimmie that he was right. He said: "You see, the potatoes help to keep LIFE in little children. So the farmer must do everything in his power to keep the potatoes growing.

"Now look at the mother and the children coming into the potato field.

"Why do you think the mother and the little boy and girl are coming into this field?"

Anna Mary said: "The mother is carrying a pitcher, so I think they are bringing the men a cool drink."

Jimmie's father asked: "And what are the children doing?"

Jimmie answered: "I think they are just coming along so they can see their father and big brother."

Then Jimmie's father said: "You see, Jimmie and Anna Mary, the children have LIFE in them, or they would not be able to come to see the men.

"The mother has LIFE in her, or she would not be able to bring a cool drink to the men.

"And it was God who gave LIFE to this father, this mother, and these children.

"God gave LIFE to you, Anna Mary. And He gave LIFE to your father and mother.

"God gave LIFE to you, Jimmie. And He gave LIFE to Mother and me.

"For, as I have told you, God loves little children, and He knows they need fathers and mothers to take care of them."

Jimmie said: "I like this story best of all."

Then, before Jimmie's father and mother and the children left the potato field, his mother said: "Now you know how good and wonderful God is.

"So, let us, each one, say a little prayer praising God because He is so wonderful and so good."

Then Anna Mary, and Jimmie, and Jimmie's father and mother said a little prayer to God.

I will tell you the prayer Jimmie's mother said:

THE PRAYER JIMMIE'S MOTHER SAID

Music: Sister Hunkele

Dear God, how good You are to give LIFE to all things on earth that live; LIFE to each bird, LIFE to each tree, And LIFE to those I love, and me.

Let us learn this prayer.

After Jimmie's father and mother, and Jimmie and Anna Mary had each said a prayer telling God how good He is, they walked to their bus.

On their way home, Jimmie and Anna Mary said: "This big field would be a good playground."

Jimmie's father said: "Yes."

Then Jimmie's father said this rhyme for them:

THINKING OF GOD WITH LOVE

Music: Sister Hunkele

God made a play-ground of the earth where ev'-ry child can play. So let us think of Him with love, when we're out-doors to-day.

After Jimmie's father had said this nice rhyme, Jimmie's mother asked the children if they would like to say it together. And both children said: "Yes."

Find the picture in your Activity Book showing that the grown-up people and the children have LIFE in them.

Color your own page.

(*pages* 22, 23)

UNIT TWO

Aim

To Develop in the Little Child

(A) An Appreciation of the Truth That in Addition to His Physical Life, God Has Given Him Another Kind of Life, i. e., the LIFE of His Intellect and Will

(B) Facility in Praying and in Practicing Virtues

MORE STORIES ABOUT TREES, FLOWERS AND VEGETABLES

LET us begin today with **THE PRAYER JIMMIE'S MOTHER SAID.**

Now look at the next pictures in your Activity Book.
(page 24)

You see that they are about trees, flowers and vegetables.

Notice the books hanging on the branches of the tree.

The picture is trying to show that the tree is reading a book.

Now you know that before you are able to tell the stories in your Activity Book, you have to think about the pictures. And you have the power to think about the tree and the books hanging on its branches, or any other story in your Activity Book.

God gave you this power to think.

But God did not give the tree the power to think.

So why is it that the tree could not think and tell about the story in the picturebook as you can?

Look at the picture of the flowers. What do you see in the midst of the flowers?

The flowers have LIFE in them and they are very beautiful.

But do you know whether God gave the flowers the power to think? Yes or no — which?

Can the flowers read the book?

Tell why you are sure that the flowers can **not** read the book.

* * *

Look at the picture of the vegetables.

There are blocks resting upon the vegetables.

But to build a house with the blocks, the vegetables would have to think.

Now, you tell me why the vegetables would never be able to build the house.

* * *

A STORY

Once upon a time I knew a little boy named Billy.

And when Billy looked at these pictures of the tree, the flowers and the vegetables, he made up a rhyme.

Would you like to hear Billy's rhyme?

BILLY'S RHYME ABOUT TREES, FLOWERS AND VEGETABLES

Music: Sister Hunkele

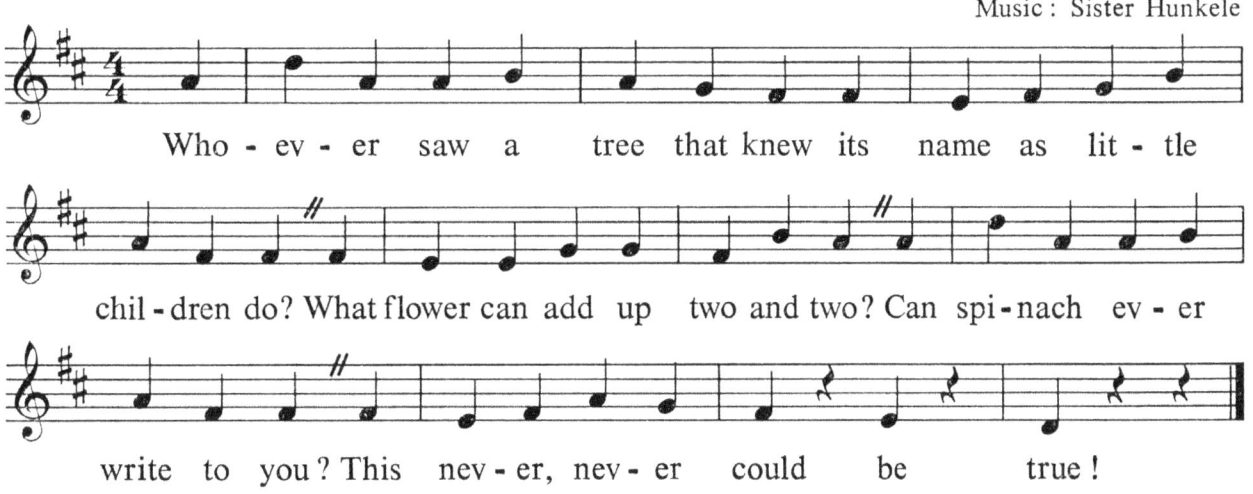

Who-ev-er saw a tree that knew its name as lit-tle chil-dren do? What flower can add up two and two? Can spi-nach ev-er write to you? This nev-er, nev-er could be true!

Shall we sing **BILLY'S RHYME** together?

* * *

Now color your own page in your Activity Book. (page 25)

MORE STORIES ABOUT ANIMALS

L ET us begin by saying the rhyme THINKING OF GOD WITH LOVE.

The next page in your Activity Book is about animals. Find it, and look at the dog in the picture. (page 26)

What does the picture tell us that the dog is trying to do?

You know that you have the power to think about the pictures in your book, and tell their stories.

But could the dog do this?

We all like the dog because he is a good playmate.

But do you suppose that boys and girls would ever take their dogs with them to school, so that they could learn to read lessons from books, as you will soon be able to do?

* * *

Look at the horse in the picture.

What is the horse trying to do?

The horse in the picture is trying to read. But do you know anyone who has ever seen a real horse reading?

We like horses because they are beautiful and useful.

But would anyone ever think of having a school for horses?

* * *

Look at the chicken in the picture.

What is the chicken trying to do?

As you say, the chicken in the picture is trying to write. But anyone who writes a story has to first know the story.

Can chickens know stories as you do?

* * *

Look at the bird in the picture.

What is the bird trying to do?

Yes, the bird in the picture is trying to draw. But no matter how hard the bird tries, will it ever be able to draw a picture?

Why couldn't the bird draw a picture?

* * *

Look at the fish in the picture.

What is the fish trying to do?

You are right. The fish in the picture is trying to play the piano. But could the little fish ever learn to play the piano, even if it tried all day long, every day?

Why couldn't the little fish learn to play the piano?

Now let us take turns in telling the story each picture shows.

One day a little boy called John was looking at pictures of many different animals.

As John looked at the pictures, he thought and thought. And at last he said this rhyme:

JOHN'S RHYME ABOUT THE ANIMALS

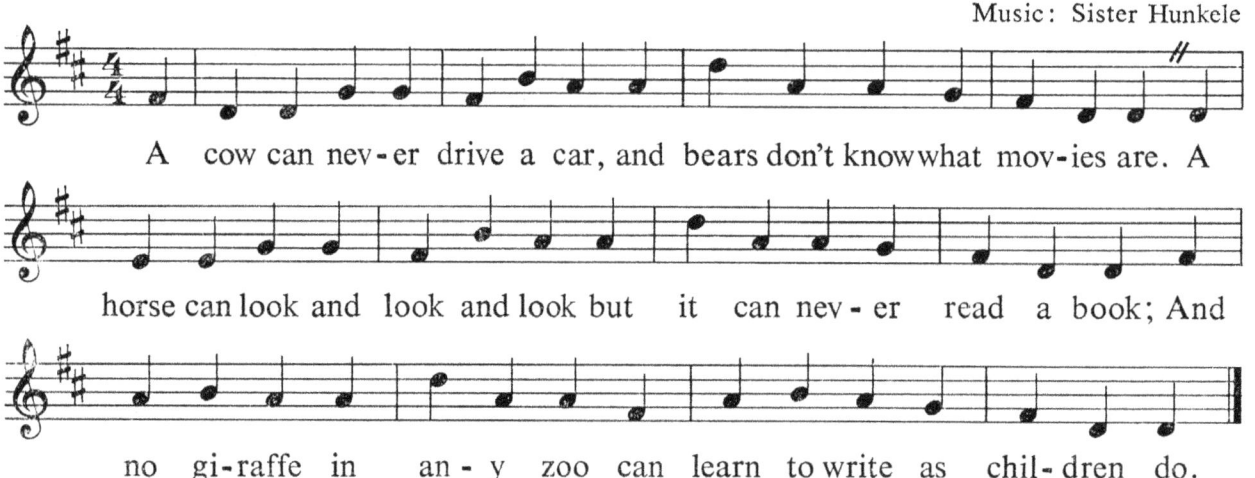

A cow can nev-er drive a car, and bears don't know what mov-ies are. A horse can look and look and look but it can nev-er read a book; And no gi-raffe in an-y zoo can learn to write as chil-dren do.

Do you like JOHN'S RHYME ABOUT THE ANIMALS?

Do you want to say it with me, line by line?

Now color your own page in your Activity Book. (*page 27*)

MORE STORIES ABOUT PEOPLE

WE WILL begin by saying the rhyme DANIEL'S QUESTION.

Look at the next pictures in your Activity Book.

(*page 28*)

These pictures are about a girl, a boy, a mother and a father.

What is the girl doing?

What is the boy doing?

What is the mother doing?

What is the father doing?

Act out one thing that can be done by boys and girls, but never by animals, birds or fish; act out another thing of the same kind.

Now tell something done by a boy or a girl, but never by an animal, a bird or a fish.

All this tells us that a boy or a girl, a mother or a father, can know how to read and write and play the piano, and draw, and do many other things.

For a girl, a boy, a mother and a father can THINK.

One day long ago, a mother was teaching her little boy about THINKING. She told him that, if he wanted to, he could THINK about different things.

The little boy's name was Joseph.

Joseph said: "It's fine to be a boy and have the power to THINK."

His mother said: "Yes, Joseph, I am glad you are able to THINK.

"So make up a rhyme to say to Father."

This is:

JOSEPH'S RHYME

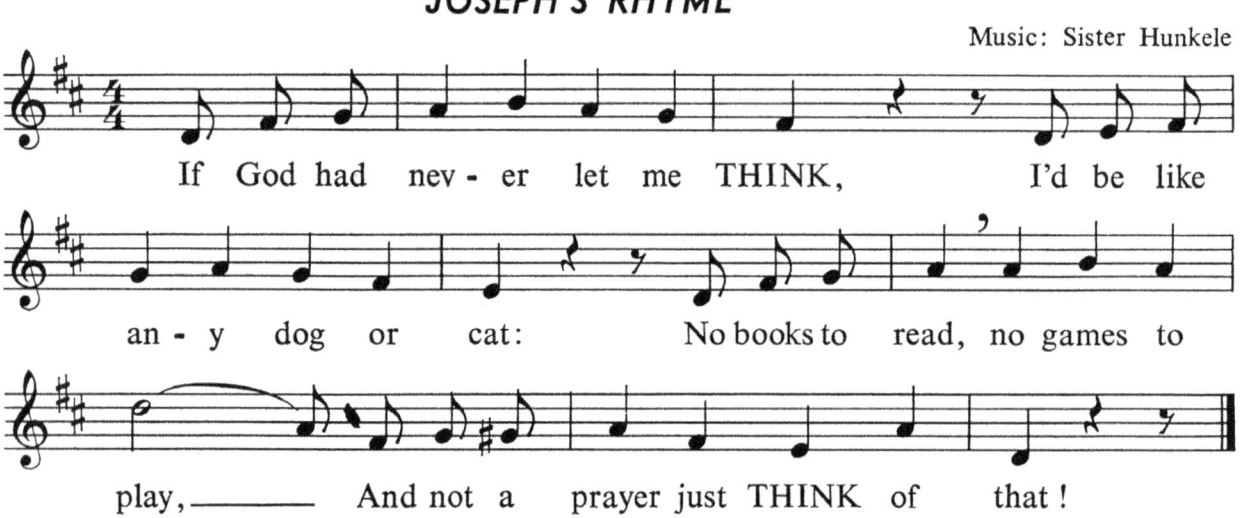

Music: Sister Hunkele

If God had never let me THINK, I'd be like any dog or cat: No books to read, no games to play, And not a prayer just THINK of that!

If you would like to say JOSEPH'S RHYME to your father, we will learn it.

Turn to the page in your Activity Book and color your own pictures.

(page 29)

TALKING TO GOD

FIRST of all, let us see if we can say MOTHER'S PRAYER.

Turn to the next picture in your Activity Book, showing three children. (page 30)

What do you think the children in the picture are doing?

You know that trees and flowers and vegetables can never learn about God or talk to Him.

And you know that dogs and ponies and bunnies can never learn about God or talk to Him.

The children cannot see God, but they can talk to God, and God knows all that the children are saying to Him.

God loves every child. He wants to give every child many good things. That is why God wants every boy and girl to talk to Him, and thank Him, and tell Him about everything.

So you see, God wants **you** to talk to Him. When you talk to God, you are PRAYING.

When I was a little girl, my mother taught me a nice rhyme about PRAYING to God. Would you like to have me say that rhyme to you?

A RHYME MY MOTHER TAUGHT ME WHEN I WAS A LITTLE GIRL

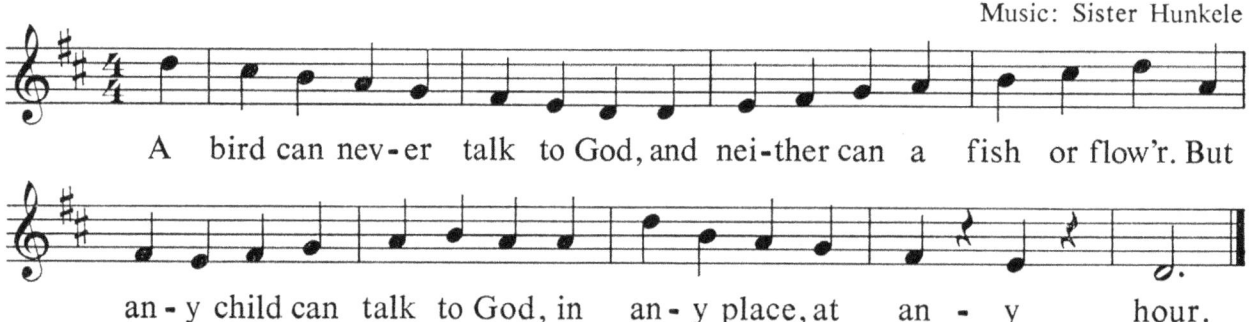

Music: Sister Hunkele

A bird can nev-er talk to God, and nei-ther can a fish or flow'r. But an-y child can talk to God, in an-y place, at an-y hour.

Do you know two special times when everyone should be sure to talk to God?

In the morning we say "Thank You" to God for having taken care of us all night long.

And we ask God to bless us and our fathers and mothers and all those we love. We ask Him to help us to be good all day long.

At night we say "Thank You" to God for having taken care of us through the day, and for helping us to be good.

And we again ask God to bless us and our fathers and mothers and all those we love.

Would you like to hear how I tell God:

MY PRAYER

Music: Sister Hunkele

O my God, Bless my fa-ther, Bless my moth-er,* Bless ev'-ry one I love, Bless me.

*At this point other blessings can be added to the same melody as the two previous measures.

Now turn to your Activity Book and color your own page about PRAYING.

(page 31)

MORE STORIES ABOUT CHILDREN

YOU know that only girls and boys and men and women can read and study, write and talk.

Today I want you to know something else that only men, women and children can do.

Here are three pencils. Choose (that is, pick out) the one with the sharpest point.

Here are three pictures. Choose the one that tells about God.

Here are two flowers. Choose the one that is yellow.

Three times I have asked you to choose. And each time I asked you, you did choose.

But if I had asked the birds, or the fish, or the animals to choose these very things, could they have done it?

Then, besides thinking, and reading, and writing, what have you just learned that children can do?

* * *

Now look at the pictures in your Activity Book.   *(page 32)*

The boy in the picture is choosing. What is he choosing?

The girl in the picture is choosing. What is she choosing?

The man in the picture is choosing. What is he choosing?

The woman in the picture is choosing. What is she choosing?

Now tell this story about what boys and girls, and men and women, can do.

In your Activity Book, color your own page about choosing.
(page 33)

* * *

When I was a little girl, Elaine was my playmate.

So one day when I was visiting Elaine, her mother told us about CHOOSING, as I have told you.

Elaine's mother said: "The power to CHOOSE is one of God's best gifts to you and to me."

Then she asked each of us to make up a rhyme about CHOOSING, and to say the rhyme to her.

Would you like to hear **ELAINE'S RHYME?**

ELAINE'S RHYME

Music: Sister Hunkele

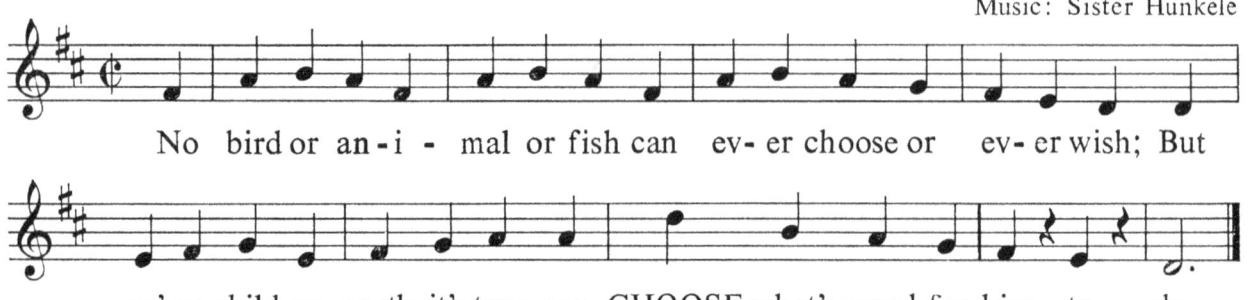

No bird or an-i-mal or fish can ev-er choose or ev-er wish; But ev'-ry child on earth, it's true, can CHOOSE what's good for him to do.

Shall we learn this rhyme?

* * *

CHEERFUL OR SULKY — WHICH?

In your last lesson you learned something that you can do which is very important. What is it?

Turn to the next page in your Activity Book. *(page 34)*

The children who are shown in this picture are choosing.

Some children are CHOOSING to be cheerful.

And other children are CHOOSING to pout or to be sulky.

Which are the cheerful children?

Which ones are not cheerful?

God, who gave LIFE to all of these children, expects them to be cheerful.

And cheerful children make many other people happy.

The children who are pouting or sulky are doing what God does not want them to do. And they make those they love unhappy.

If someone had a camera and took the picture of a boy or girl who is sulking, do you think the boy or girl would like to see the picture?

If you felt like being sulky, what would you do?

It is hard to be cheerful all the time.

But when a child is cheerful even though he does not feel like it, he shows that he is thinking about the best thing to do, and CHOOSING it.

Turn to your Activity Book and color a picture showing cheerful children. (page 35)

Pretend it is your picture, and tell the story about being cheerful. I will write it for you.

ORDERLY OR DISORDERLY — WHICH?

You have been learning that all children and all men and women have the power to CHOOSE.

So each one of us can CHOOSE to do what God wants him to do, or he can CHOOSE to do what God does not want him to do.

Turn to the next page in your Activity Book. *(page 36)*

The children who are shown in this picture are choosing.

Some children are choosing to be orderly. Everything is in the right place.

But there is one child choosing to be disorderly. Nothing is in the right place.

Which child is choosing to be disorderly? Which ones are choosing to be orderly?

If you want your home to be beautiful and happy, you must help by being very orderly.

All that God does is orderly. And God wants all children to be orderly also.

So God wants you to be orderly.

Tell the story you have learned about being orderly and disorderly.

✸ ✸ ✸

Color a picture in your Activity Book showing orderly children. *(page 37)*

Then, if you let me know the story you want your picture to tell, I will write it.

KIND OR SELFISH — WHICH?

We have been having many lessons, telling about one thing that children can do which is very important. What is it?

Turn to the next picture in your Activity Book. *(page 38)*

The children in the picture are choosing.

Some are choosing to be kind and helpful.

And one is choosing to be unkind and selfish.

Which one is choosing to be unkind and selfish?

Which ones are choosing to be kind and helpful?

You know that God is always kind, and that God is always doing kind acts.

And God, who gave LIFE to all children, expects them to be kind to each other.

Name some kind acts that a child can do.

Tell what you have learned about being kind.

Color a picture in your Activity Book showing kind children.
(page 39)

* * *

Shall I write what you told on the Activity Page?

GENEROUS OR GREEDY — WHICH?

Look at the next picture in your Activity Book. *(page 40)*

In the picture the children are choosing.

You see that one child is choosing to share a toy with a playmate. We say that such children are generous.

Another child is choosing not to give any candy to a playmate. We say that such children are greedy.

Which children do you like better — the ones who are generous, or the ones who are greedy?

Children who want to be happy, and also to make others happy, must be generous, and never greedy.

Tell what some greedy children do to other children.

Tell what you can do to show that you are not greedy.

* * *

Color a page in your Activity Book to show a child being generous. *(page 41)*

UNIT THREE

Aim

(A) To Make Jesus, God's Own Son, Known to the Little Child

(B) To Inform the Child Concerning the New Life Received at Baptism

JESUS IS GOD'S OWN SON

THERE is a picture in your Activity Book showing the Very Best Person who ever lived in this world.

Let us look at this picture. *(page 42)*

Do you know His Name?

We call Him JESUS.

This picture shows us JESUS when He was about as old as you are.

Before JESUS came to this earth, He always lived with God His Father in another world called Heaven.

God loves you, and your father and mother, and all the other people of this world very, very much. And because He loves us, He wants everyone to be good.

That is why He sent His Own Son to live on earth as you and I do.

For JESUS knew what we must do to be good, and when He was no longer a little Boy, but had grown to be a Man, He told all the people He met how to be good men and women.

These men and women told other men and women what JESUS had said.

And, at last, it was written in books, so that we could know about it.

JESUS loved God His Father, and was always thinking of Him. He talked with His Father a long time every day, and a long time every night.

He prayed to His Father to help Him make people everywhere kind and gentle.

And, of course, JESUS Himself was always kind and gentle.

JESUS was kind and gentle even with people who were not good to Him.

And JESUS' Father was always well pleased with HIS OWN BELOVED SON.

* * *

Now JESUS is not living upon this earth as we do.

He is in Heaven with His Father.

But even though JESUS is in Heaven, He knows when we are talking to Him, and all that we say.

And JESUS wants us to talk to Him every day. For He loves us, and if we ask Him, He will give us all that we need to be good and happy.

Now whisper a little prayer to JESUS.

* * *

Let us see if you have heard the story well enough to answer some questions.

1. Whose Son is JESUS?

2. Before God's Own Son came to this earth, where did He live?

3. Why did JESUS' Father send Him to live upon this earth?

4. Some people are rough and unkind. Others are kind and gentle. Which was JESUS?

5. We cannot see JESUS now, because He is in Heaven with His Father. But does JESUS know when we talk to Him?

6. What must we do if we want JESUS to help us and do good things for us?

7. See if you can tell this story about JESUS without any help.

* * *

Would you like to have a picture of JESUS to hang in your room?

Color the picture on the right page in your Activity Book.
(page 43)

THE BABY JESUS

YOU know about the Best Person who ever lived upon this earth. Who was this Person?

Tell one story you have learned about JESUS. Another story. Another story.

* * *

Does the next picture in your Activity Book show JESUS as a little Boy about as old as you are, or as a tiny Baby?
(page 44)

Have you a picture showing how you looked when you were a tiny baby?

Do you like that picture?

Which picture of JESUS do you like better — the one showing Him as a little Boy, or the one showing Him as a tiny Baby?

Would you like to know something about JESUS when He was a tiny Baby?

JESUS came to this earth a long, long time ago.

And even when He was a little Baby, JESUS knew what all the people on the earth were doing.

For, you see, JESUS was always GOD, just like His Father.

When you were a little baby, did you know what all the people in the world were doing?

No other baby except JESUS could do this.

And now I shall tell you why JESUS was much greater and more important than any other baby. This is the very best story in all the world.

* * *

JESUS IS GOD

Even when JESUS was a Baby, He saw that some of the people were not doing right. They were bad.

And JESUS wanted very, very much to have all the people good and kind like His Father.

So His little Heart was sad when He saw that the people were not doing right.

As I have told you before, JESUS came to earth to show people the right way to be happy. The right way to be happy is to be good.

So, even when JESUS was five, like some of you, He asked His Father every day to make people good.

Now see if you can answer these questions:

1. Even when JESUS was a tiny Baby, why was His little Heart sad?

2. Why was JESUS greater and more important than any other baby?

3. Whom was JESUS like?

4. What did JESUS ask His Father every day?

* * *

Turn to your Activity Book and color your own picture of THE BABY JESUS. *(page 45)*

JESUS' MOTHER

YOU have been learning a story about JESUS when He was a little Baby.

And you know that God is Jesus' Father. But we cannot see Jesus' Father because He never came to live upon this earth as Jesus did.

But JESUS had a Mother who lived upon this earth, as your mothers do.

So I know that now you want to hear a story about **JESUS' MOTHER**.

First, look at the picture of Jesus' Mother shown in your Activity Book. (page 46)

We call JESUS' Mother THE BLESSED VIRGIN MARY.

God asked a very holy man to take care of the Blessed Virgin Mary and Little JESUS when He came to live upon this earth.

This holy man's name was SAINT JOSEPH.

One day, Joseph and the Blessed Virgin Mary left their home to go to another town, called Bethlehem, on some important business.

The Blessed Virgin Mary and Joseph were obliged to stay all night in a cave where some animals were kept, for Joseph was poor.

While they were in the cave, THE BABY JESUS came to earth. So the Blessed Virgin Mary laid THE BABY JESUS in the manger where the animals used to eat.

Perhaps you went to the church on Christmas Day to visit the Crib, and saw the little statue of the ox and the little donkey right next to THE BABY JESUS.

But if you have never visited the Crib with THE BABY JESUS in it, I am sure you will do this next Christmas and every other Christmas as long as you live.

As I have told you, THE BABY JESUS is GOD, so He could choose His own Mother. He chose the Blessed Virgin Mary.

She was very, very lovely.

You know that JESUS and His Mother are now living in the other world called Heaven.

They will live in Heaven forever.

JESUS loves His Mother.

And JESUS wants us to love His Mother.

I always pray to her every day, and I think you, too, will like to pray to JESUS' Mother every day.

Perhaps you would like to say this prayer to her:

A PRAYER

Music: Sister Hunkele

O Blessed Virgin Mary, I love you! Please pray That I may be more and more Like Jesus ev'ry day.

* * *

Shall I read the story again, or do you remember it?

I will ask you some questions. See if you can answer them.

1. Who was the only Child Whose Father never lived upon this earth?

2. Who is JESUS' Father?

3. Who is JESUS' Mother?

4. Tell what you know about JESUS' Mother.

5. What holy man took care of THE BABY JESUS and His Mother?

6. When THE BABY JESUS came to this earth, where did His Mother lay Him? Why?

7. Where are JESUS and His Mother now?

8. The story tells every boy and girl to love the Blessed Virgin Mary. Who wants us to love her?

* * *

Color your own picture of Jesus' lovely Mother.

(page 47)

JESUS, THE GOD-MAN

JESUS was always praying to His Father for everyone. And when JESUS became a Man, He spent three years going from place to place, teaching the people how to be good, and telling them about His Father in Heaven.

Look at the picture of JESUS when He grew to be a Man.
(page 48)

Because God is JESUS' Father and the Blessed Virgin Mary is His Mother, JESUS is called the GOD-MAN.

Many people loved to listen to JESUS when He was teaching.

And JESUS told the people that if they wanted to be very good, they must first of all love His Father more than anybody or anything.

Then they wanted to hear more about JESUS' Father. So they followed JESUS from place to place.

And most of those who followed Him tried very hard to be good. For they loved JESUS and wanted to be more and more like Him.

One day, the people following JESUS were very tired and hungry.

There were five thousand people. Five thousand means many, many people. They had nothing to eat at all but seven loaves of bread and a few little fishes.

JESUS took the seven loaves of bread and the few little fishes and prayed.

Then, right away, there was plenty of food to feed all the five thousand people.

JESUS was always kind and good to all the people who asked Him to help them.

Many men and women who were sick came to ask JESUS to cure them. When JESUS just touched these sick people, they were well again.

JESUS even put life into people who were dead. For He was God, and the power of God was in Him.

* * *

Now see if you can answer some more questions about our story.

1. When JESUS grew to be a Man, He told the people about Someone very great and good. Who?

2. What did JESUS tell the people they must do, if they wanted to be very good?

3. Tell some kind deeds JESUS did for the people.

4. Why did the people who followed JESUS try very hard to be good?

* * *

Without questions, see if you can tell the story about JESUS.

Would you like to have me read you the story again?

Now I will tell you one more thing about JESUS, and you will like to hear it very much:

JESUS loved little children.

And when the mothers brought their little children to Him, He put His hand upon their heads and blessed them.

One day, when JESUS' friends knew that He was tired, they wanted to send the little children away from Him.

But JESUS only brought the little children closer to Him.

And He told His friends that they must never send them away from Him. For He liked to have them near Him.

This made the children very happy.

And all these little children loved JESUS.

* * *

See if you can answer these questions about JESUS:

1. Because JESUS is God and also Man, what is He often called?

2. JESUS did good things for all the people who came to Him. But which ones did He love very, very much?

3. When their mothers brought the little children to JESUS, what did He do for them?

4. When some of JESUS' friends wanted to send the children away, what did JESUS tell them?

5. What will JESUS do for you, if you love Him very much?

6. Try to tell the story about JESUS, THE GOD-MAN, without any questions from me.

* * *

Look in your Activity Book for the picture of JESUS blessing little children. Color your own picture. (*pages 48, 49*)

SOME STORIES ABOUT JESUS, THE GOD-MAN

Would you like to hear a few stories telling of the good things JESUS did for different people?

The stories are all found in a book called the Bible, so they are true stories.

For all the stories in the Bible are true.

The first story is about Lazarus.

LAZARUS

Long ago, there was a man called Lazarus.
And Lazarus was very sick.

Lazarus had two sisters. One was called Martha. The other was called Mary.

JESUS was in another town when Lazarus became sick. So Martha and Mary sent a message to JESUS, saying, "Lord, the one whom You love is sick."

You see, Martha and Mary called JESUS "Lord."

And when Martha and Mary said, "The one whom You love," they meant Lazarus. For JESUS loved Lazarus very much.

Now you tell what Martha and Mary said to JESUS.

JESUS also loved Martha, and her sister Mary.

But it was several days after He received their message before He came to their house.

Then the people told JESUS that Lazarus had been so very sick that he had died. He had NO LIFE in him.

Now he was in a grave. He had been there for four days without any LIFE in him. And Martha and Mary thought they would never see their brother Lazarus again.

When Martha met JESUS, she said: "Lord, if You had been here, my brother would never have died."

Then JESUS said to Martha: "Your brother will rise again."

When Mary met JESUS, she said to Him, just as Martha did: "Lord, if You had been here, my brother would never have died."

"Master" means "Lord."

When JESUS saw Mary crying, He was sorry for her, and He said very kindly: "Where have you laid him?"

Martha and Mary said: "Lord, come and see."

JESUS wept, and went to the grave where Lazarus was buried.

What does "JESUS wept" mean?

When JESUS and Martha and Mary and the other people were standing by the grave where Lazarus was buried, JESUS prayed to His Father.

After that, JESUS said in a loud voice:

"Lazarus, come out!"

Then all the people were surprised. They could not believe what they saw.

For Lazarus rose right up from his grave. He was ALIVE again, and he could talk to JESUS and Martha and Mary and all the other people.

Martha and Mary were very happy then.

For JESUS had shown His power.

(Saint John 11:1-45)

And this means that JESUS had such power that He could do what no one else could do.

* * *

See if you can answer these questions:

1. What book tells many stories about JESUS?

2. Tell the name of the man in the story who had NO LIFE in him.

3. Tell the names of his two sisters.

4. Tell in your own words what Martha and Mary both said to JESUS when He came to their house.

5. What did JESUS do when He came to the place where Lazarus was buried?

6. What did JESUS say in a loud voice?

7. When JESUS spoke, did Lazarus keep on being dead, or did he become ALIVE again?

8. No one on earth ever had so much power as JESUS had. Now JESUS is in Heaven. But can He help anyone just the same?

* * *

Wouldn't you like to tell your father or mother or playmates about Lazarus?

TWO BLIND MEN

Have you ever seen a boy or girl who was blind?

There are many blind boys and girls in the world. They cannot see anything.

The story today is not about blind boys and girls, but about two blind men.

JESUS had been teaching the people.

He was going to another place, and a great crowd was following Him.

Two blind men sat by the roadside.

The blind men, of course, could not see, but they heard the people say, "JESUS is passing by."

Then the blind men called out:

"Lord, have mercy on us!"

The people told the two blind men to keep still. But the blind men called out all the louder:

"Lord, have mercy on us!"

Then JESUS stood still, and said to the blind men:

"What will you have Me do for you?"

They answered Him:

"Lord, that our eyes be opened."

After the blind men had asked JESUS to use His power and cure their blindness, JESUS touched the blind men's eyes.

Then all the people were surprised at what happened. For at once the blind men could see.

Do you not think that the blind men were very, very happy then?

JESUS had done what the blind men had asked Him to do.

He had shown His power.

Then the blind men went with the other people who were following JESUS.

(Saint Matthew 20:29-34)

* * *

Tell the story of the blind men by answering these questions:

    1. How did the two blind men know that JESUS was passing by?

    2. What did the blind men call out to JESUS?

    3. When the blind men called out to JESUS, what did the people say to them?

    4. What did JESUS do to the blind men's eyes?

    5. When JESUS touched the blind men's eyes, did they remain blind? What happened?

Now tell the story of the two blind men without any questions from me.

THE RULER'S LITTLE DAUGHTER

Have you ever seen the ocean? a lake? a river? a pond?

Have you ever played or walked by the seashore?

* * *

One day when JESUS was standing near the seashore teaching a multitude of people, a man came running up to Him.

The man's name was Jairus.

And Jairus was a ruler. Today we would call him a governor.

When Jairus came up to JESUS, he told JESUS that his little daughter was very, very sick.

He said that he was even afraid she would die.

JESUS felt sorry for Jairus.

So JESUS told Jairus not to be afraid, but to believe in Him and in His power.

These are the very words JESUS said:

"Do not be afraid, only have faith."

Now you tell what JESUS said to Jairus.

JESUS went to the house where Jairus and his little sick child lived.

There were many people there crying. They were crying because the little girl no longer had LIFE in her.

JESUS said to all these people:

"Why do you make this din, and weep? The girl is asleep, not dead."

Then the people laughed at JESUS, because they thought He did not understand that the little girl had NO LIFE in her.

But they did not know that JESUS had more power than the doctor or the priest or any other person.

JESUS paid no attention to the people who were laughing at Him. He took the little girl by the hand and said to her:

"Girl, ... arise."

And at once the little girl rose up and began to walk.

Then JESUS told her father and mother to give the little girl something to eat.

(Saint Mark 5:21-43)

Can you answer these questions?

1. Who are some rulers in our country?

2. The ruler called Jairus had a little daughter. What was the matter with her?

3. JESUS was sorry for the ruler. So what did JESUS say to Jairus?

4. When JESUS went to the ruler's house, what were most of the people doing?

5. What did JESUS say to the little girl?

6. Then what did the little girl do?

7. What did JESUS tell the little girl's father and mother to give her?

THE CRUCIFIX

You have learned that JESUS, THE GOD-MAN, was very, very good and kind. For He was like His Father.

And you know that He wanted all people everywhere to be good and kind.

But many people were not good and kind. They were very bad.

And when JESUS told these bad people that He was truly God's Own Son, they wanted to kill Him.

At last, some bad men nailed JESUS to a big cross. And they left Him there until there was NO LIFE in Him.

JESUS' Mother and some of JESUS' friends stood by the cross weeping and praying.

But even though the bad people hurt JESUS so much, and left Him to die on the cross, **JESUS did not hate them.** He loved them, and He felt sorry that they were so bad.

He even asked His Father to have mercy on them.

Look at the picture in your Activity Book. Notice the cross. Whose Image is nailed to the cross? *(page 50)*

A cross with an image of JESUS' Holy Body on it is called a Crucifix.

And all people who love JESUS like to have a Crucifix. It helps them to remember that JESUS died upon the cross because He loved all people and wanted to make them good.

Would you like to have a Crucifix in your room?

See if you can answer these questions about JESUS' death and the Crucifix:

1. What did bad men do to JESUS?

2. How did JESUS act toward these bad men?

3. What did JESUS ask His Father to do for them?

4. What is the shape of a Crucifix?

5. Whose Image is nailed to the cross?

6. People who love JESUS like to have a Crucifix. Why do they?

* * *

Color a page in your Activity Book showing a Crucifix.
(page 51)

For your story, tell JESUS that you love Him.
Have Mother or Father write your story.

JESUS IS ALIVE!

JESUS died on Good Friday but He promised the people that He would rise again. Jesus kept His promise. On the first Easter Sunday, Jesus rose from the dead.

Now Jesus had a new life, a risen life. This was the kind of life He wanted for all of us. Jesus rose from the dead to give us this new life. Jesus stayed on earth for many days to show His apostles that He had this new life.

On Ascension Day the apostles watched Jesus go up to Heaven to live with His Father forever. Before Jesus went back to His Father He promised to send us another Friend.

    1. What did Jesus promise the people He would do after He died?

    2. How did Jesus keep this promise?

    3. What kind of life did Jesus have when He rose from the dead?

    4. Why did Jesus stay on earth for many days?

    5. What did Jesus do on Ascension Day?

JESUS SENDS THE NEW FRIEND

TEN days after Jesus went back to His Father in Heaven, He sent the new Friend. This new Friend is the Holy Spirit. He will live with us forever.

The Holy Spirit gives us the New Kind of Life which Jesus had when He rose from the dead.

1. Who was the New Friend whom Jesus sent?

2. What does the Holy Spirit give us?

KINDS OF LIFE

WHEN we began our lessons, you learned that boys and girls have ONE KIND OF LIFE in them that lets them walk, and run, and jump, and swim, and laugh, and talk.

Act out three of the things that boys and girls can do when they have this kind of LIFE in them.

A little later you learned that there is A SECOND KIND OF LIFE boys and girls have. And because they have this kind of LIFE in them, they can read, and study, and learn, and choose.

Act out two things that you can do because you have this kind of LIFE in you.

Which kind of LIFE do you use when you want to know more about God — the first kind of LIFE, or the second kind?

* * *

The next lesson is almost the last one in the book. It is a very important lesson, because it tells about A THIRD KIND OF LIFE that God gives us.

BAPTISM

JESUS died and rose from the dead to give us this THIRD KIND OF LIFE.

God gives us this LIFE when we are BAPTIZED.

Unless we have this kind of LIFE that God gives us at BAPTISM, we never can be as good as God wants us to be.

You have been BAPTIZED.

When you were a little baby, you were carried to the church. Those who brought you to the church went to the BAPTISMAL FONT. Then the priest came there to BAPTIZE you.

When you are a little older, I will tell you more about your BAPTISM.

But now I want you to know that the kind of LIFE you received at BAPTISM is the best of all.

For then God drew you closer to Himself and the HOLY SPIRIT came to live with you.

God wants you to pray to HIM. This new kind of LIFE which God gave you when you were BAPTIZED helps you to pray. And it also helps you to get to HEAVEN.

Now I will ask you only two questions. But they are very important.

1. **Tell what God gave you when you were Baptized.**

2. **Why is the new LIFE God gave you at Baptism the best of all?**

* * *

One day last summer I invited my class of little boys to go with me on a picnic.

First we took a long boat ride. And after that we rode on the streetcar to a nice shady park, where we ate the lunch we had carried with us.

Then we walked around the park looking at the trees, and flowers, and doves, and sheep that were there.

While we walked, the boys talked about THE THREE KINDS OF LIFE that God had given to us.

I cannot remember the rhyme said by every boy. But I can remember Jerry's and Peter's rhymes.

This is:

JERRY'S RHYME

Music: Sister Hunkele

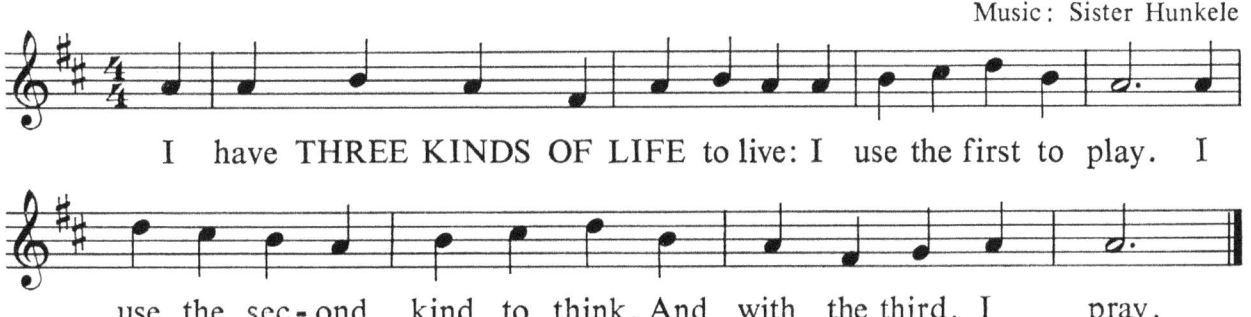

I have THREE KINDS OF LIFE to live: I use the first to play. I use the sec-ond kind to think. And with the third, I pray.

Do you like **JERRY'S RHYME**? Shall we learn it?

Now would you like to hear:

PETER'S RHYME

Music: Sister Hunkele

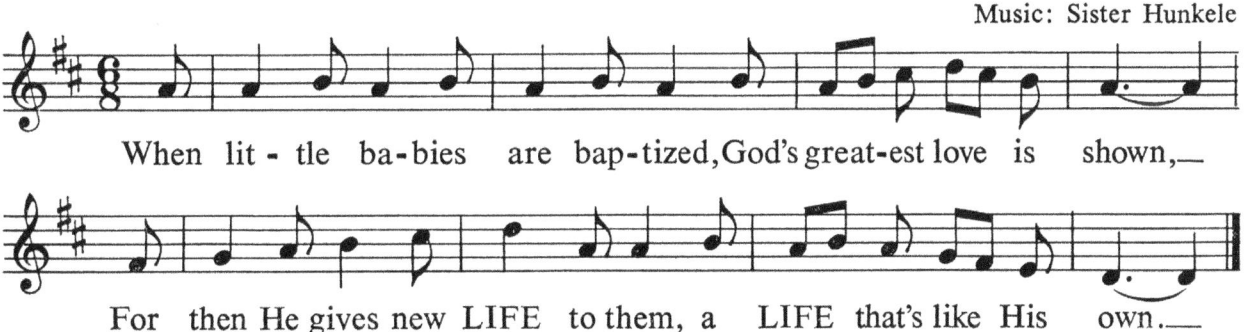

When lit-tle ba-bies are bap-tized, God's great-est love is shown,— For then He gives new LIFE to them, a LIFE that's like His own.—

Shall we learn **PETER'S RHYME**?

Turn to your Activity Book. Look at the picture telling about Baptism.

Color the page in the Activity Book that shows Peter's rhyme.

(*pages 52, 53*)

THE CHURCH WHERE JESUS LIVES

JESUS is not living upon this earth as He did long ago. Now He is in Heaven. But you know that you can talk to Him at any time and in any place. And JESUS will always hear you.

There is one very special place where many people like to talk to JESUS.

That special place is the Church where JESUS lives.

And whenever your mother or father or your nurse takes you to **THE CHURCH WHERE JESUS LIVES,** you should talk to Him there.

You can tell Him that you believe He is God's Own Son.

You can tell Him that you love Him.

You can thank Him for letting you go to His Church to be Baptized.

And, like the people of long ago, you can ask Him to do good things for you, for your father and mother, for all those you love, and for anyone else for whom you would like to pray.

Find the picture in the Activity Book showing THE CHURCH WHERE JESUS LIVES. *(page 54)*

* * *

Here are some little prayers that you may say:

"Dear JESUS, I thank You for all the good things You have done for me."

"Dear JESUS, I want to be kind and good like You. Please help me."

"Dear JESUS, bless me as You did the little children long ago."

"Dear JESUS, I am sorry the bad men hurt You so much."

"Dear JESUS, I will always love Your Mother, the Blessed Virgin Mary."

* * *

Make your own picture of THE CHURCH WHERE JESUS LIVES. *(page 55)*

www.ingramcontent.com/pod-product-compliance
Lightning Source LLC
Chambersburg PA
CBHW081348040426
42450CB00015B/3350